THE DOLLY LLAMA

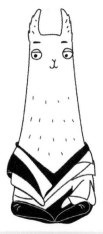

Words of Wisdom from
a Spiritual Animal

STEPHEN MORRISON

STERLING
New York

STERLING
New York

An Imprint of Sterling Publishing Co., Inc.
1166 Avenue of the Americas
New York, NY 10036

This Sterling edition published in 2019. First published in Great Britain by Michael O'Mara Books Limited.

ISBN 978-1-4549-3476-9

For information about custom editions, special sales, and premium and corporate purchases, please contact Sterling Special Sales at 800-805-5489 or specialsales@sterlingpublishing.com.

Manufactured in China

2 4 6 8 10 9 7 5 3 1

sterlingpublishing.com

Designed by Jade Wheaton
Illustrated by Ja Cię Broszę

For llama Mave

Special thanks to James Menzies,
Tom Whiteley and Yonel Osman.

About the Author

His Gentleness the **DOLLY LLAMA** is the spiritual leader of most even-toed ungulates in the Andes, Peru and some parts of Bolivia.

He has devoted all twenty-seven years of his life to working tirelessly to help teach the findings of Llama Karma to alpacas, camels, Bactrian camels, wild Bactrian camels and, of course, llamas. Today he lives in exile, on a petting farm in Dulwich.

STEPHEN MORRISON is a man from the north of England. In the past, he has worked seasonally as a bee negotiator as well as a swan whisperer. This is his first work as a spiritual llama interpreter.

Contents

An introduction to Llama Karma with the Dolly Llama

As sentient mammals, we all want to be happy and avoid suffering. In my years travelling the world in a stock rack on the back of a Nissan Frontier, I have learned that to achieve this we need to cultivate the mind. It all starts up here. You can't see me doing it right now, but I'm pointing to my mind. Good.

The Llama Karma tradition to which I belong, teaches that the best way to keep a happy mind is through 'cuditation' (a hybrid of meditation and chewing).

Cuditating can sometimes mean standing in a field and chewing cud blankly in a figure-eight jaw movement for so long that you accidentally 'mark your territory' without realizing. Yet it can also involve finding time to repeat to oneself the positive teachings of a deeply nurturing practice.

I speak of the ancient dharma passed down from mammal to mammal as selflessly as the camelid cow expresses milk from her udders. It is for this reason that the practice was named 'Uddism'.

Llama Karma is the deliberate energies, thoughts, actions and facial expressions that have been guided by Uddist wisdom. Involuntary and unconscious actions such as night emissions or blinking off a fly do not constitute Llama Karma.

I have drawn great inspiration from the Uddist 'Four Bales of Wisdom'; teachings that have helped many grazer-browsers before myself to find a lasting peace on the rocky path of life.

These Bales contain much useful advice on compassion, discipline, transmigration, and not hoofing out about the future or the past. They teach us that we must counsel ourselves to always consider other camelids to be more important than ourselves (even the guanaco, a wild breed of llama who never break eye contact and so always get into fights).

These hay scriptures confirm that only through discipline may we constantly cultivate the fields of our mind. Only then may we become beasts of unburden.

They conclude that by not hoofing out about the future or the past, we can remain in the 'llama present'. This frees us from regret (such as guilt about our browser history), whilst also unshackling us from our deepest fears (such as being overpowered by any of the big cats).

This offering that you hold in your hooves or hands contains daily quotations from these ancient scriptures, as well as some other invaluable mammal mantras that I have nurtured on my travels.

It is with these that I continue on my journey towards finding Llama Nirvana, a level of enlightenment so capacious that it causes the tail to stick up and the hind legs to quiver upon reaching. I thought I had found it two summers back when I licked an electric fence.

I humbly pray that you too, regardless of your genus, may draw some inspiration from these wisdoms to develop that warm-hearted peace of mind that is key to enduring happiness.

I also pray that you never get pulled to the ground by a guanaco.

Deepest Gentleness,
The Dolly Llama

CHAPTER 1

Compassion

It is the nature of llamas to yearn for freedom, dignity, and foliage on demand. If we accept that others are entitled to peace and happiness and leaf rights equal to our own, do we have a responsibility to those in need? Yes. The answer is yes.

The more you care for the happiness of camelids, the greater is your own contentment. Therefore, llama compassion or 'Llama Amour' should never change, even if those in your pack behave negatively.

Compassion is expressed through thought and action as well as in every purr, whinny, and hum. All of us have the emotional intelligence to display it at all times—even the guanaco have this ability (and they eat AstroTurf—genuinely).

To understand compassion, we must learn that it is an emotional response as well as a rational one, in the same way that a tree can also be your friend as well as your dinner.

Even more importantly, having an inner compassion means everything will be fine, no matter the adversity we face.

Three summers ago, I shared a paddock with a herd of South African Dorper during the worst drought in thirty years. Many farmers had lost entire crops and the herd was worried about how all this was going to affect 'them'.

It was my task to try to keep these sheep calm whilst they got on with their own important job of augmenting their nation's fiber industry.

One member of my flock suffered an optical strabismus, a condition that left her with a wandering eye and earned her the name 'Steve Buscemi'. She was a deeply troubled creature who felt the internal pressure of not fitting in as well as the external pressure we all shared . . . the pressure of the relentless blazing sun.

It had taken Steve Buscemi a long time to come to me for help (largely because she was poor at judging distances) and by the time that she did, she'd become so distressed that she was now almost comically cross-eyed.

Thankfully, I was able convince this ewe, so troubled with her eyes, that with compassion there is never really a 'you' and there are no 'I's', and that it was essential for her to try to look outwardly and not inwardly. In fairness, this may have only confused her more, but it is a truth all of us must embrace if we are to find peace.

You will be pleased to hear, of course, that just as all things in life are subject to change, in time those South African skies did open. And it was a life-affirming sight to see Steve Buscemi lapping gratefully from a puddle, along with the rest of the herd.

Let us now take a cleansing breath, sit comfortably (or remain standing if you are a horse) and enjoy the cuditations of the first of the four Bales, along with some invaluable lessons I have learned during my time as a llama.

Cuditations
of the 'Bale of
Compassion'

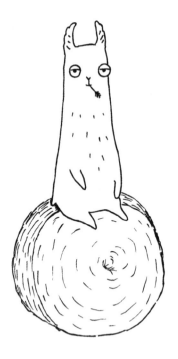

To wherever you travel
In sun or in rain
Keep the side window
Of compassion
Wound fully down
And always have
At least one appendage
Hanging out of it
For it will comfort you greatly
To know you that you
Have exposed yourself
To kindness

Choosing a religion
Is like choosing
Which open-top haulage vehicle
To be driven around in

It may be the church
Of the Chevrolet Avalanche
The shrine of the Nissan Frontier
Or the temple of the
Renault Alaskan . . .

Yet as long as you remain
On the path to tranquility
It matters not
what you travel IN

Although the chrome bars
On an Isuzu D-max
Will take your teeth out
Like a backstreet dentist
Every time

Compassion is an udder disinfectant
When sprayed it reaches out
To all in the pack
Even those without infection
Even those without udders

Neither wind nor fire
Can erase our good deeds
Not even a really bad fire
Like when Goat Paul
Put his head in the Aga cooker
Because he 'wanted A sausage'

Llamas are social animals
Who sometimes like
To ascend the mountain
Bunched one behind the other
And have a furry conga
Which is fun
But requires the cooperation
And assistance of everyone
For it to work . . .

It is better to have no companions
And be a conga train of one
Than it is to be with one llama
Who does not care
About the effect their reckless
Cornering is having
On the back of the conga line
And yes, Gerard
This is one hundred percent
Aimed at you . . .

Lose your hump if you have one
Bitterness and resentment
Are empty calories
And are about as nourishing
As AstroTurf

If you are a llama with fighting teeth, get them extracted by an animal dentist. That way you will know you cannot cause harm* to anyone you are pastured with.

If you are not a llama, get your fighting teeth removed figuratively by a metaphorical dentist.

* Apart from chest ramming

Let your mind be as free of ill thought
as your wool is free of lanolin.

Lanolin is wool grease and grease will
cause you to slip.

If you spit at a llama
And they don't spit back
Know that later on
They will spit at a llama
They consider weaker
Than themselves
And that this weaker llama
Will in turn
Find an even weaker
Llama to spit at
Probably one with a wry face
Or asthma . . .

On and on this will go
Until the tiniest, frailest
Runtiest llama
Has been spat at
Right in the face

Remember this well
For to bully one
Is to bully all

The most important lesson is to know good thoughts from bad. With that in mind, let us try to work out which of the thoughts below are positive and which thoughts promote ill will:

'The grass is resplendent'
'The berries are delicious'
'The rain is renewing'
'That bridle comes near me one more time, Stuart, and you'll need a go-cart wheel for a leg'

Compassion is by its very nature
Peaceful and gentle
But it is also powerful
Like a dove
In a high governmental position

Building paddock fences
Can exclude us
From those who are
Our brothers and sisters

If you must build any fence
Let it not be barbed with prejudice
Or tall with ignorance . . .

Let it be a fence you can still see
your brothers and sisters over
No more than four feet high
And with a three-sided shelter
To provide shade and protection
From extreme heat

Give freely of your wool
Every three years
So that others can
Snuggle in its warmth
Rather than hang
Onto it for so long
That you look like
A cloud with teeth

It is very rare or almost impossible
that an event can be negative from
all points of view.

Though the time Gerard spat at that
old lady on a mobility scooter would
come close.

Hatred cannot be overcome
By hatred in the same way
An owl cannot be eaten
By the same owl

It is as easy for a rich camel
To pass through the eye of a needle
As it is for the rest of us to
Negotiate a cattle grid

Drink deeply of the milk
Of compassion
Do not drink from the paint cans
We found in the far field

Gerard drank four of them
And went so mad that
For a short while
He thought he was a bird

If you think you are too small to make
a difference, try sleeping with a mosquito.

If you can get past the obvious logistical
issues, it will do wonders for your
self-confidence.

CHAPTER 2

Discipline

Each of us already command some level of discipline in our daily lives. Without it we would not be able to keep our jobs as load bearers or sentry guards put in place to reduce predation of sheep, goats, and hens.

It is told that llama were domesticated more than two millennia ago. Before then, they were base, wild, and dirty, a lot like the guanaco. This is mainly because back then they were guanaco, given that the guanaco are undomesticated llama. Of course, the guanaco regard the llama as over-privileged versions of themselves, believing us to be obsessed with fence prices and being in a decent paddock catchment area. The guanaco are entitled to their opinion like every living creature is, but given that I once saw one try to sleep with a see-saw, I know which species my money is on.

Just as the llama can be domesticated and calmed and culturally advanced, so too can the mind. The first step towards achieving inner peace is to endeavour to practice. Indeed, the path towards tranquillity is not an even one. There will be days when cuditation comes easy to us, but on the bad days we must practice too. The days when we are so troubled by our surroundings that the small oblong patches on each side of our rears emit alarm pheromones, causing disquiet in the herd—these are the days on which we need to cuditate the most.

It is only with such devotion in place that we can develop good Llama Karma, then move forward and free ourselves from unimportant distractions such as bark binges and fetlock management.

It is through discipline that we manage thankfulness and through a thankful heart that we arrive at enlightenment. Once we are here, nothing can trouble the lake of peace that runs within us.

As a case in point, let us take my friend Lord Plough. Lord Plough is a show llama so focused on his own brand that he has little time for anything else, although I still count him as a friend.

When I ask Lord Plough what he values most in life, he tells me it is his rosette for halter record in the Best Heavy Woolled Young Male category. I then remind him this award is not permanent and that one day another heavy-woolled llama will hold the title. Lord Plough claims that when that day comes he will go for the same award but in the 'older male' category. I tell him this is all very well but that this bauble too will not be a permanent one. He tells me he is well aware of that, and when the day comes where he loses that title, he will request to be put out to stud. I ask him what makes him think he will be selected to stud at such a venerable age, at which point he reminds me that his name is Lord Plough.

Despite his ambitious nature, Lord Plough's life is perilous because it is one of obsession and attachment. In his pursuit of this lifestyle, Lord Plough has made a rod for his own back.

The cuditations in this chapter, therefore, will not only affirm the importance of setting goals for improvement, but also show that cuditation is not biting off more than you can chew. I hope you will hum and click peacefully along with them.

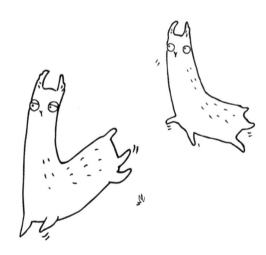

Cuditations of the 'Bale of Discipline'

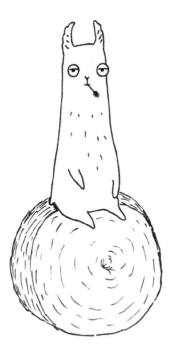

Discipline is something we practice, just as we practice getting up those mountains with the bad gradients. (The ones that even goats can't deal with).

Some days we will be up for the climb, and on others we will not be feeling it. Just as with those mountains we must reward ourselves for every time we do try, and forgive ourselves when we slip.

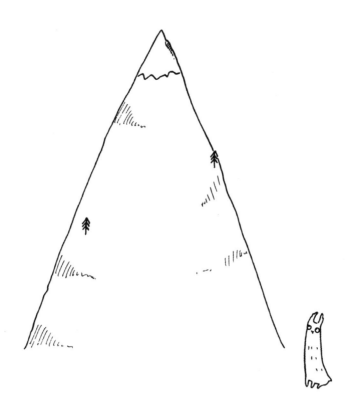

I'd rather walk 10 miles with a 50-pound bag on my back, than 20 miles with a 25-pound bag. This is not a metaphor, just experience. The vet said he had never fitted a hernia belt to a llama before.

The goal is not to be better
Than any other
But to be better than
Your previous self
And definitely to be better
Than Lord Plough
Although given that he has
Now started accessorizing
With ear tassles
This is a pretty low bar

See that your temper
Is as evenly attached
As your saddle pad
If not, the imbalance
may cause irritation
And cause you to rear up
And everything you carried
So well that day
Will be lost to the mountain
And potentially covered
In hawk poop

A llama has two hums
The hum of contentment
And the hum of deep concern
Let yours be the hum
Of contentment
And not the hum of concern
Even though both hums
Sound identical
Which is a bit of a design flaw
To say the least

The very purpose of our life
Is to seek happiness
This can come from simple pleasures
Such as gazing up at the stars
Or for the less sophisticated guanaco
From something as simple
As ramming a rival mate
When he's not looking

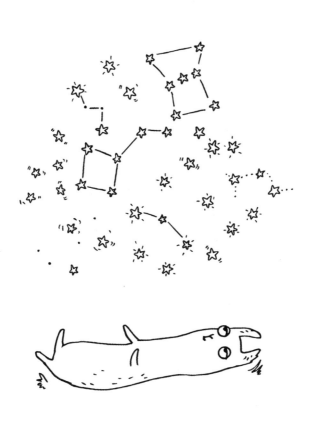

Gaze into a muddied lake
Now gaze into a weed-strewn lake
And gaze into a final lake
One stirred and agitated by wind

You will not see your long face
In any of these lakes
Even though it is there

The mud is doubt
The weeds are sloth
The wind is agitation

For it is when we fail
To see what mires us
That we are at our most lost

And when we are able to gaze
Into this many lakes
In such a short space of time
That we are in Finland

Patience is the most admirable
Of virtues in all creatures
It is the ability
To press on through

The repetitive
The anticipated
The expected
The foreseeable
The certain
The discernible
The conspicuous
The calculable
The conspicuous
The indisputable
The recognizable

The perceptible
The conclusive
The manifest
The unsubtle
The interminable
The unvaried
The wearisome
The unexciting
The spiritless
The characterless
The monotonous
The irritating
The trying
And the upsetting
Without reward

The most important thing in life
Is to simply put one foot
In front of the other

Move forward in life
With this simplicity
Unless there's a mountain lion
In which case, strike off with
The non-leading hind foot
Quickly moving the legs
In unison in diagonal pairs

To develop patience, spend time with the guanaco. Such a beast gives a real opportunity to practice tolerance.

For anything that spends an entire evening dry heaving whilst repeating the words 'bad twigs', will test your inner strength more than any Guru could ever do . . .

Patience protects us from being discouraged, and when it comes to bark binges the guanaco will never learn to find its own level.

Do not want for more
Remember when Big Consuela
Jumped over the fence
And ended up falling into that lake
In the belief it was
The Great Blue Afterlife
That was embarrassing
For all involved

Adapt to bad attitudes
Like you do to bad altitudes
Use your extra red blood cells
To tolerate them
Don't let anyone exhaust you

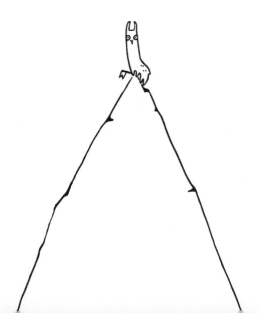

Your saddle pack is like your mind
Burden it only with the bare necessities
As you begin your daily trek . . .

Ask yourself:

Does anyone really need this
Extra can of stove fuel?
These two small cook stoves?
These pots and pans?
These extra gloves in a ziplock bag?
These matches dunked in wax?
This space blanket?
These wet wipes?
These plastic insulated cups?
This framed print of a clown
Flipping a pancake?
This tuba?

Since even humans can gradually
Be trained with patience
The llama mind can also be
Trained step-by-step

It is good to vary the diet
A change from
Llamaian cuisine (bark and grass)
Can be a good thing
Some nights you should go
Sheep (grass)
Alpaca (grass)
Goat (grass bark, plants, and peel)
But never Fox (anything in garbage bag)

Tolerate ungulates
Of all colors
Whether they are black
White, brown
Reddish brown
Reddish brown with mottled
patches of yellow and white
Or piebald

Discipline is a supreme ornament
Worn round the neck like a bell
But the bell makes no sound
And is not an actual bell
Regardless, when worn
It gives birth only to happiness
Despite it being
(And I can't stress this enough)
Not an actual bell

CHAPTER 3

Transmigration, Hope and Rebirth

For those new to the practice of the dharma of Uddism and Llama Karma, often the greatest sticking point is coming to terms with a belief in transmigration.

Many rear up anxiously at the concept just as they would a farmer approaching their pen with a worming needle.

But just as we can accept 5ccs of Dectromax in the neck as long as we are approached properly (from behind, with the needle at a low gradient and the injector moving with us), so too can we accept the principle of transmigration.

Transmigration is where the sentience of a creature transfers to another body after death. As such, Uddists do not fear death. For instance, I am dictating this introduction whilst guarding a hen farm in Paraguay and I have just heard what I think was a low guttural growl. There may be a cougar trying to get into the coop, which is fine because I do not fear death.

Uddists prefer the term transmigration to reincarnation because it contains the word 'migration', which is something all creatures enjoy (apart from the Chinook salmon, but then if you will insist on swimming 900 miles against strong river currents to get back to your spawning ground, you're just creating your own admin).

Uddists believe that as well as the self transferring at death, it also renews every moment, meaning that nothing about the self continues from one moment to the next.

By the way, I just heard the growl thing again and I'm now 90 percent certain it was just the wind making the barn creak, which is great, but it would also have been fine if there was a cougar as I'd have dealt with that, but it's great that it probably now isn't a cougar.

We believe that the whole of creation is in a constant fluctuating state. Energies within our bodies have their own power to grow within a new form, independent of the previous form or identity. Anyway, cougars are hissers and don't tend to growl, so I'm guessing when I patrol over there in a while (which I will do) I'll find we're thankfully well out of the woods on this one.

Uddists have believed for centuries that there is no permanent, unchanging element that continues. We must strive to be better or we risk returning and repeating our mistakes again in this life or a lower one.

I hope this chapter will help assist you to that end. It contains the Bale wisdom on the cycle of change as well as my own thoughts on the importance of hope and emotional rebirth and acceptance.

Cuditation
of the 'Bale of
Transmigration,
Hope and Rebirth'

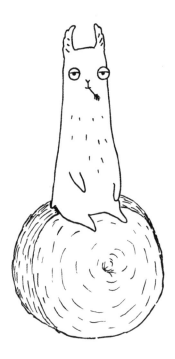

You are your own master
Absolutely everything
Depends on you

Sorry, that was meant
To sound empowering
And inspiring
Rather than stressful

The soul never truly dies.
The body never truly lives.

In some shape or another, one always exists.
Although the jury is out on slugs.

Just one small positive thought
In the morning can change
Your whole day

I start every day thinking
About the time Goat Paul
Bit into a helium balloon
So hard one of his eyes
Changed color

Death is not to be feared
By someone who has lived wisely
Which would explain
Why Lord Plough
Is so thoroughly petrified
Of death

A youngster once asked me
If reincarnation truly exists
Then why do wasps exist
And I'll be honest
I didn't have an answer for him

Hopeful thoughts are like
The llamas of North America
During the last ice age

They may appear to have been
Wiped out totally
But thirteen millennia later
They will be reintroduced
By private animal collectors
And zoos

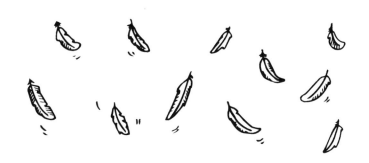

Life is sacred, savor it.

In other news, I just watched Marcus, a pheasant, three fields along, run headlong into a combine harvester in the belief that it was his long-lost, heavy-set uncle.

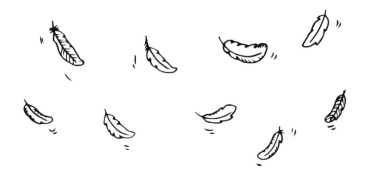

Today we were visited by a large group
of schoolchildren.

I hope in my next life I am reborn as something
without ears, like a snake or a brick.

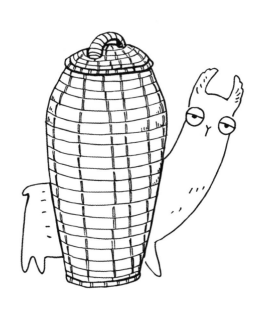

Today let us imagine hope
Is a fly trying to land
On the flared nostril of a camel
For a nice bit of warmth

The camel snorts the fly away
The camel swooshes the fly away
The camel is having none of it . . .

Soon the fly will die
Then by the by
Be reborn
As a slightly bigger fly
Bent on nostril action

So it goes
On hope grows
Incrementally bigger fly
To exactly same-sized nose

All things are subject to change
Even change itself
For one day
Change itself will change
To unchanged
Meaning no things will be
Subject to change
But only for a short while
And just for a bit of a change

We are born and reborn many times
(Usually with our mother standing up)
As such we are connected
By the familial

All of us have been
Each in our turn
The infant
The parent
And the high-voiced aunti
With the hoof infection

Spying a high blossomed branch
You may stretch for it
Leap for it
As doubters hum and bray . . .

Undeterred you leap higher
Until finally you manage to make contact
With the branch's lowest finger
With great effort you
Drag your leafy purchase
to the ground
Using your neck muscles

Soon the branch is picked bare
Everything changes
Beauty turns to ugliness
Hunger into satedness
And triumph into a realization
That there was a similar
blossomed branch
At eye level

CHAPTER 4

Not Hoofing Out About the Future or Past

As grazer-browser animals, we have always been beset with indecision. Choosing whether to graze or browse is the most operative of these, but we also worry about the path behind us as well as the path before us. It is possible to fear both; sometimes fearing one can make us lament the other and it isn't long before our banana-shaped ears go back and the next thing we know we be hoofing.

I should point out that while llamas, like other species, sometimes get into such a colossal flap that we begin braying and slamming our hind legs into whatever or whomever, this would not accurately be called 'hoofing', since as ungulates we are not possessed of hooves. I have used 'hoofing' in this context for the purposes of brevity since 'not padding out with two toe bones embedded in a broad cutaneous pad about the future or past' would have been a bad heading. I'm also sorry about writing 'we be hoofing'. I have just spent an evening in Lord Plough's stable, or 'crib' as he calls it, and I think this has made me temporarily urban. It is *so* not me to say 'we be hoofing', just as it is *so* not me to say 'so not me'. I *so* need to spend less time with Lord Plough.

Indeed, the past and future can be the subjects of obsession. But, like the guanaco's temper, the past is already lost and, like the guanaco's charisma, the future is not yet here. There is only one moment in which to live and that is the present.

Perhaps the eldest and best-known servant to the dharma of Uddism was the Venerable Dromedary camel cow 'Mammal Cass', who lived through the tenth-century collapse of China as well as a turnip blight.

Cass, a four-chambered stomach ruminant, would regularly regurgitate her findings so that they could be broken down into teachings that even the simplest of camelids could grasp. The following famed quote was recorded by a Vicuna scribe in 940 AD:

'If you want to know your past, look at your present. If you want to know your future, look at your HUUUUUUUURK! I'VE BEEN STUNG BY A WASP! AN ACTUAL WASP ON MY TOE FLAP! HUUUUUUURK! GOD IT HURTS SO MUCH! WHY DIDN'T ANY OF YOU TELL ME? WHY DIDN'T ANY OF YOU TELL ME THERE WAS A WASP?'

Since Cass perished shortly after this statement, succumbing to what turned out to be the fatal sting of a sweat bee, scholars have perused the text for centuries in the hope of finding its full meaning and most are almost 90 percent certain that she was about to confirm that the future, like the past, is governed by the present.

The present is the key to all peace. It is the sheep dog that gently flanks the herd of the mind, pushing it up to the pen.

With that in mind, I think this chapter of cuditations will be invaluable to all of us, and will help us avoid any unwanted internal events, including self-llaming and alpacanic attacks.

I trust they will bring you peace.

Cuditations
of the 'Bale of Not Hoofing Out About the Future or Past'

Most llamas are never fully present
As they chew on their bark
Because unconsciously they believe
The next bark must be more
Peaty than this one
But then they miss their whole life
Trapped in a barky peat quest

Imagine a hen

Happiness is a leaf blowing
In a storm
Chase it and you will not find it
Let it come to you
And then eat it
Just to be sure

Happiness can be found
Even in adversity
Like when Big Consuela found
An apple grove while being
Chased by those dogs
Big Consuela loves an apple

If you abandon the present moment
You cannot live in the moments
Of your daily life deeply

If you abandon your
Personal hygiene
To the extent that even
Ticks avoid you
You are Gerard's grandma

Mindfulness isn't difficult
You just need to remember to do it
A bit like remembering to fake
A munge infection
On the day
A school party is visiting

We can no more change the past
Than we can reduce the
Amount of shoplifting
That goes on in the farm gift shop
Although nobody steals the
Massive pencils
As they're difficult to conceal
And in my opinion
Just an impractical gimmick

You cannot catch a Frisbee
In your mouth
By worrying about where
That Frisbee has been
Or lamenting the future
Of the Frisbee industry

Often it is better to do something
Than not to do it
I have seldom felt lasting regret
For anything that I've done
Even the time I licked that frog
And got so high I tried
To climb into a poster

Everything you try to hang onto
Will eventually become lost to you
Even the 'Superdry' hat
You had off that kid's head
Will eventually be prised
From your jaw
Although it will take three
Staff members to manage this
And the front of the hat
Will read 'Su'
By the time that they do

There are two llamas in our group who are both called Eddie. One of them is obsessed with running ahead and sniffing everything and the other is more of a sitter downer.

It is when our mind acts like restful Eddie and not 'spray everything like a dog' Eddie that the miracle has happened.

The next message you need in life
Is always right where you are
My ex Linda was always right
Where I was also
But to be fair
She had abandonment issues

Nothing remains as it was
If you know this you can begin again
With pure joy in the uprooting
Like an indecisive camping couple
With a penchant for taking down
And repitching their tent

Yesterday I saw a crow

To worry what others think of you
Is to vainly ponder your future
To live in the now
With calm, kind focus
Is to be what you always would
wish to be to all others

I told Lord Plough this the other day
But he was too busy eyeing up
An Appaloosa short hair
Over my shoulder . . .

I think he just comes out with me
So he can chat up females
Without looking weird by being
Out on his own
Honestly sometimes
I don't know why I bother

Beware the path to the past
As well as the path to the future
These paths are full of shale
And really slippery
And are NOT REAL PATHS

A female llama when pregnant
Will spit at her mate
Whenever he approaches
To remind him she is pregnant

So too must we spit
At thoughts of the future
And thoughts of the past
Whenever they approach us
To remind them we are present

If both toenails on our feet
Are pruned too short
We will wince as we cover rocks
If they are left to grow too long
We will stagger on stony ground
And make an annoying clacking sound . . .

Our thoughts
Like our toenails
Must be coiffured to be the
Right length for the now
Not over-shorn by worry
Nor in lament be left curling
Back on themselves

CHAPTER 5

The Essential 'Mammal Mantras'

As a twenty-seven-year-old, I am often asked what the secret is to my longevity. Indeed, living by a Llama Karmic code has certainly been key to this, but I have also taken great strength from using the Uddist mammal mantras.

A mammal mantra is a sequence of self-affirming words or sounds, chanted, often repetitively, by any animal who is part of the practice of Uddism.

The function of a mammal mantra is to evoke enlightenment; even though this light can be somewhat rudimentary and stifled in many species.

For example, a guanaco's one single affirmation is so basic it literally translates to 'Here!', which effectively means that throughout its entire life the guanaco is persistently answering some kind of internal roll call on which only the guanaco's name is listed.

During my time being a llama, I have studied the proclamations of most mammals and have been comforted greatly by many soothing bleat assertions and woof litanies as well as the promise of the cow.

It is, however, the invocations of my own genus that I have found to be the most enlightening. These mantras are known as Holy Llamifestations, or 'Llama Calmers' if you are trying to reach a younger crowd.

These Holy llamifestations are easy to grasp and each is as empowering as a bowl of Kellogg's Start©*.

I offer them to you along with the information that straw or shredded paper makes excellent bedding in a windproof enclosure.

*Sadly discontinued

Mountain Mantra

Mountain Mantra is often used to help overcome mental or emotional blockages, along with physical ones, such as shearing rash.

Mountain energy is active and soothing and steps down to help all camelids in strife, from the sunburnt cria to the noble Suri alpaca, tethered and way out of its depth, trying to ward off a mad horse.

The only thing required for this mantra to work is that we need to let go and cease our clinging to a particular outcome, as we would to a thin ledge on a mountain, because to cling to a particular outcome is often self-defeating, and can lead to some serious hoofing. The more we have the noble mountain's non-grasping attitude; the happier we are.

When chanting the Mountain Mantra, we need to let go and bring the energy back into ourselves. This will generate immense inner peace and clarity.

Meaning of the
Mountain Mantra

Lead me from illusion to reality
Lead me from the darkness to the bright
Lead me from end to beginning
Let there be peace, peace, peace

Pronunciation in llama
'SKREEEEEEEEEEEEEEEEEEEEEEEEEE!'

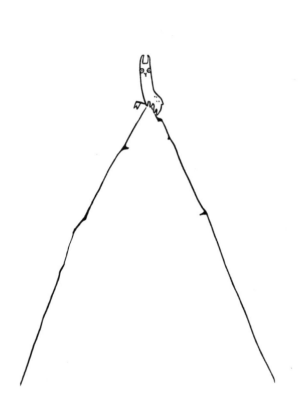

The Pure Sky Mantra

Pure Sky Mantra is used to help achieve success. Since we are regularly overtaken on the trail and want to get back to the front, we need to recite this mantra every day. It can help us gain the success and inner happiness being at the front brings, as well as eliminate the problems, unhappiness and suffering caused by being at the back or middle.

The highly exalted Dolpopa Padmasambhava (a llama so wise he completed his enlightenment during his own gestation period) believed that if you recite the Pure Sky Mantra at the time of death you would be reborn no lower than a carriage pony in status. To confirm, that's a carriage pony or above.

Meaning of the Pure Sky Mantra

——————— *ɩɩɩɪʋɩɩɩɩ* ———————

Hail, appear O leader, great leader,
your word teaches us that it is acceptable
to expand our horizons and lets us find
prosperity and success in this life

——————— *ɩɩɩɪʋɩɩɩɩ* ———————

Pronunciation in llama
'SKREEEEEEEEEEEEEEEEEEEEEEEEEE!'

CHAPTER 6

Hemootat the
Silent Brother

The Silent Brother is known to be the mute spirit of the first of the llama. He is said to take the form of a prehistoric paleo-llama, which is similar to a modern llama only with a shorter and much less complex large intestine.

In animal lore, Hemootat* transcends continents as well as faiths. In the kingdom of ungulates he is known by many names and titles, including the All-Camel, Breaker of Gates, Mighty Listener, Dune Reaper and Fat Carl.

Yes, and no prizes for guessing which species of undomesticated llama uses that last one.

The Silent Brother's mantra helps us to gain access to the irrepressible unseen energy that he symbolizes. He is invoked by beasts of burden who seek reinvigoration and inclusion. A young llama left out of the team in a game of 'bite the beanbag' might be wise to invoke the silent warmth of Heemootat.

*Hemootat is even acknowledged as a prophet in the bovine faith of Cowism, only here his name is pronounced with a silent H, a silent E, a silent T, a silent A, and a final silent T.

Just like his nature, Hemootat's mantra is non-vocal. Instead, the 'invokee' is to stand on soft land pulling an expression of mild disapproval.

Then the Silent Brother will enter your heart and stand nobly by your side, and you will be replenished by the affirmation that a llama may stand alone and be connected to the universe, just as that conversely, a llama may stand with many other llamas and constantly bleat on about all the rosettes he has won, the amount that he earns, the size of his stable and ear tassels, yet still experience what I can only imagine is a deep, deep detachment and bitter loneliness.

Many thanks for traveling this far with me. We have learned a great deal together.

That a good life is a kind one. That to make mindfulness a habit is a true honor. That moment of life must be savored such that we can enjoy the next.

And that the guanaco are so stupid they believe airplanes that pass above them to be 'really confident crows'.

I leave you with my blessing and wish you a long three decades of life.

Baamaste,
The Dolly Llama